PRECIOUS MOMENTS

R He Is
Risen

Lauren
GIVEN TO

Easter
OCCASION

_4-15-01_
DATE

> ## "Why do you seek the living among the dead? He is not here, but is risen!"
>
> Luke 24:5b–6a

As that first Sunday morning dawned, so did the hope of all God's creation. Jesus, who had been crucified for our sins was now risen from the dead, His work of salvation complete for those who call on His name. What a glorious time for celebration! This Easter, before the baskets are plundered and all the eggs found, we hope that *He Is Risen* will provide your family with a beautiful picture of Easter's true meaning. Alongside the delicate illustrations of Sam Butcher's beloved **Precious Moments**® characters are verses that make memorizing easy. It's a simple and beautiful way to remember the love of our Lord on Easter Day — and every day.

And these words which
I command you today shall be
in your heart. You shall teach
them diligently to your children,
and shall talk of them when
you sit in your house.

Deuteronomy 6:6–7a

All we like sheep
have gone astray;
We have turned, every one,
to his own way;
And the LORD has laid on
Him the iniquity of us all.

Isaiah 53:6

He was wounded for our
transgressions,
He was bruised for our iniquities;
The chastisement for
our peace was upon Him,
And by His stripes we are healed.

Isaiah 53:5

And when they had come to the place called Calvary, there they crucified Him, and the criminals, one on the right hand and the other on the left.

Luke 23:33

And when Jesus had cried out with a loud voice, He said, "Father, into Your hands I commit My spirit." Having said this, He breathed His last. So when the centurion saw what had happened, he glorified God, saying, "Certainly this was a righteous Man!"

Luke 23:46-47

"Behold!
The Lamb of God
who takes away the sin
of the world!"

John 1:29

And behold, there was
a great earthquake;
for an angel of the Lord
descended from heaven,
and came and rolled back
the stone from the door,
and sat on it.

Matthew 28:2

"Do not be afraid,
for I know that you seek
Jesus who was crucified.
He is not here; for He is risen,
as He said. Come, see the
place where the Lord lay."

Matthew 28:5b-6

All the ends of the world
Shall remember and
turn to the LORD,
And all the families
of the nations
Shall worship before You.

Psalm 22:27

The LORD is my shepherd;
I shall not want.
He makes me to
lie down in green pastures;
He leads me beside the still waters.
He restores my soul;
He leads me in the paths
of righteousness
For His name's sake.

Psalm 23:1-3

He will feed His flock
like a shepherd;
He will gather the lambs
with His arm,
And carry them in His bosom,
And gently lead those who
are with young.

Isaiah 40:11

I was glad when
they said to me,
"Let us go into the
house of the LORD."

Psalm 122:1

One thing I have
desired of the LORD,
That will I seek:
That I may dwell in the
house of the LORD
All the days of my life,
To behold the beauty of the LORD,
And to inquire in His temple.

Psalm 27:4

Then He said to them all,
"If anyone desires to
come after Me,
let him deny himself,
and take up his cross daily,
and follow Me."

Luke 9:23

> "And these words . . . shall be in your heart . . .
> teach them diligently to your children. . . ."
>
> Deuteronomy 6:6 – 7a

When the women discovered that Jesus was risen, they
didn't walk to tell the other disciples — they ran! Indeed,
the news of Jesus' resurrection is so exciting that generation after generation has passed it on from parent to child,
and child to friend. Join in the celebra-
tion, not only this Easter, but all year
long as you rejoice in your risen Savior.
Like the women and the disciples, share
the joy you've found with others
who may have never heard the
good news of Jesus Christ. He is
risen, and His life gives us reason
to rejoice with the dawn of each
new day. Hallelujah!